P9-DNP-099

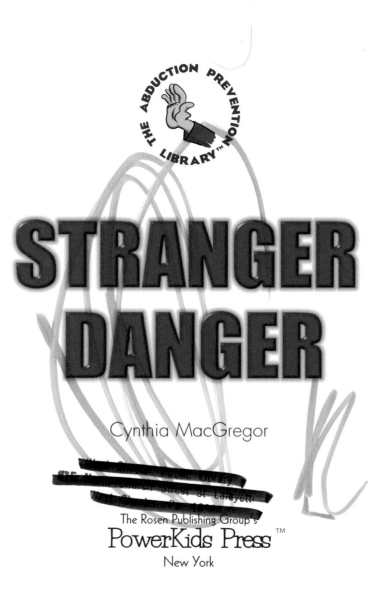

STRANGER DANGER

Cynthia MacGregor

The Rosen Publishing Group's
PowerKids Press™
New York

Published in 1999 by The Rosen Publishing Group, Inc.
29 East 21st Street, New York, NY 10010

Copyright © 1999 by The Rosen Publishing Group, Inc.

All rights reserved. No part of this book may be reproduced in any form without permission in writing from the publisher, except by a reviewer.

First Edition

Book Design: Danielle Primiceri

Photo Credits: Cover Donna M. Scholl; pp. 4, 7, 8, 12, 15, 16, 19, 20 © Seth Dinnerman; p. 11 © Phyllis Picardi/International Stock.

MacGregor, Cynthia.
    Stranger danger/ by Cynthia MacGregor.
       p.   cm. — (The abduction prevention library)
    Summary: Explains why it is necessary to be careful around strangers and offers advice on ways to stay safe.
    ISBN 0-8239-5247-9
    1. Children and strangers—Juvenile literature. 2. Abduction—Prevention—Juvenile literature.
    3. Child sexual abuse—Prevention—Juvenile literature. [1.Strangers. 2. Safety.]
    I. Title. II. Series.
HQ784.S8M37 1997
613.6'083—dc21   97-32957
                                                                                    CIP
                                                                                    AC

Manufactured in the United States of America

Contents

Meeting People

You have met many people. Most of them have been nice people. But sometimes people aren't nice. And there are a few who will want to hurt you if they have a chance.

When you first meet someone, you don't know if she is a good person or a bad person. That is why it's important to be careful with people you don't know. People you don't know are called **strangers** (STRAYN-jerz).

◄ *Any person, even if she seems nice, is still a stranger if you don't already know her.*

Who Is a Stranger?

A stranger is anyone you don't know or someone you only know a little.

All people are strangers when you first meet them. Even your best friend used to be a stranger. Most strangers are nice people. But some are not. How do you know who is a nice stranger and who is a **dangerous** (DAYN-jer-us) stranger? You don't.

It's safest and best for you not to **trust** (TRUST) any adult or older kid unless your parents or teacher say that person is okay.

Meeting and talking to strangers is okay ▶
if you're with your mom or dad.

Dangerous Strangers Play Tricks

A dangerous stranger may try to trick you into going somewhere with him or her. Don't fall for any sneaky tricks!

👋 A stranger may tell you that your mom sent him to pick you up. The stranger may tell you that your mom's car broke down or that she is sick so you'll go with him.

👋 A stranger may offer you ice cream or candy.

👋 A stranger may tell you she has lost her dog and wants you to help her look for it.

◀ *Don't trust what a stranger says to you,*
no matter how nice he or she looks.

Protect Yourself

You can protect yourself against a stranger by using your brain and your feet.

Use your brain to **realize** (REE-uh-lyz) that it's a stranger. Don't believe what the person says. For example, don't let a stranger tell you she needs your help in finding her lost pet. What's important is to keep yourself safe. If someone comes up to you and you feel **uncomfortable** (un-KUMF-ter-bul), use your feet to get away quickly. If the person follows you, yell, "Get away!" or, "You're not my father!" or, "You're not my mother!"

If a stranger is following you, go to an adult you trust. Run if you have to.

Finding Help

What if a stranger seems to be following you? Or what if someone in a car asks you to get into the car with him?

Don't try to outrun the stranger or take a shortcut where there are no people around. If you don't see a police officer, you may have to ask another stranger for help. You can ask a crossing guard, a woman who has kids with her, or someone working behind a store counter. If you don't see anyone, go to a store or house quickly and tell a grown-up.

◀ *Asking for help from a shopkeeper is a smart and safe thing to do.*

"Your Mom Sent Me"

What if your mom or dad needs to send a stranger to pick you up?

You and your family should agree ahead of time on a **code word** (KOHD WURD), such as 'kangaroo.' What if your mom sends a neighbor that you don't know well to bring you home? Your mom will tell that neighbor your code word. The neighbor will then tell you, "Your code word is 'kangaroo.' Your mom is at the dentist's office. I'll take you home." That way you know you can believe and trust her.

Once you hear your code word from a friend of your parents or your neighbor, you'll know you can trust her. ▶

Street Safety Rules

✋ If you walk to school, try to walk with a friend. It's safest walking in pairs or groups.

✋ Be **alert** (uh-LERT) and **aware** (uh-WAYR) of who is around you.

✋ Remember, bad people will sometimes look and act very nice.

✋ If a stranger tries to talk to you, say, "Sorry, I can't talk to you," and walk away. Don't even talk for just a minute. Your safety is more important than manners. And don't let a stranger get close enough to grab you. If the stranger is that close to you, run away.

◄ *Remember your safety rules and share them with your friends. Then you can all be safe.*

More Rules to Remember

✋ Never get into a car with a stranger unless he or she knows your code word.

✋ Always carry money to use at a **pay phone** (PAY FOHN). If you're lost or in trouble, you can call a parent or a family friend.

✋ If you don't have money and you need help, you can call 911, which is a free call. This phone number will contact the police.

✋ **Memorize** (MEM-or-yz) your home phone number and your parents' work numbers.

✋ Avoid using public bathrooms except when you are with a grown-up whom you trust. (The bathrooms at school are okay.)

*It's okay to use a pay phone to call for help ▶
if you feel uncomfortable or are scared.*

Home Alone

If you're home alone, don't open the door for a stranger. (Remember, this means even for people you know a little bit.) Keep the door locked. You shouldn't even open the door to see if the person has left. Talk to your parents about whether you should answer the door at all when you're home alone.

If a stranger calls on the phone, don't let him know that you're alone. Say that your mom is in the shower or taking a nap. It's okay to lie about that.

◀ *Don't worry about upsetting someone if you don't open the door. Your safety is more important.*

Relax ... But Be Careful

Remember, most people are nice and helpful people and don't want to hurt you. But there are some bad strangers out there too.

You should be careful with all strangers. You can't tell who is dangerous just by how she looks or acts.

Remember the rules in this book. Be smart and careful, and you will stay safe.

Glossary

alert (uh-LERT) Paying attention to what is going on around you.

aware (uh-WAYR) Knowing what is going on around you.

code word (KOHD WURD) A word that you and your parents agree to share with people that you all trust.

dangerous (DAYN-jer-us) Not safe; harmful.

memorize (MEM-or-yz) To learn something by heart.

pay phone (PAY FOHN) A public telephone that you put money into before you can use it.

realize (REE-uh-lyz) To become aware of something.

stranger (STRAYN-jer) A person you don't know well.

trust (TRUST) Knowing that you can count on someone to be honest and not hurt you.

uncomfortable (un-KUMF-ter-bul) Feeling scared or unsure about something around you.

Index

A
alert, being, 17
alone, being, 21
aware, being, 17

C
code word, 14, 18

H
help, asking for, 13, 18

M
memorizing, 18

N
911, 18

P
phone, 21
  pay phone, 18
police, 13, 18

R
running, 17

S
safety, 6, 10, 17
strangers
  dangerous, 6, 9, 22
  defined, 5, 6
  following you, 13

protecting
  yourself from, 10, 13, 17, 18, 21

T
tricks, 9
trust, 6, 14, 18

U
uncomfortable, feeling, 10

Y
yelling, 10